"WHAT IF..."

by
Don W. Hillis

Cartoons
by
John V. Lawing, Jr.

Reprinted by permission of
CHRISTIANITY TODAY

Published by
VICTOR BOOKS

a division of SP Publications, Inc.
P.O. Box 1825 • Wheaton, Ill. 60187

Cartoons © *Christianity Today* 1969, 1970, 1971, 1972, 1973. Used by permission. Scripture quotations are from the King James Version unless otherwise identified.

Library of Congress Catalog Card Nnmber:74-21908
ISBN: 0-88207-601-9

© 1975 by SP Publications, Inc. World rights reserved
Printed in the United States of America

VICTOR BOOKS
A division of SP Publications, Inc.
P. O. Box 1825 • Wheaton, Illinois 60187

CONTENTS

1. Some Pork Chops, Peter? 7
2. Joseph and Situation Ethics 10
3. Watch Out! Somebody Loves You! 13
4. That Problem of Priorities 16
5. Oh, for the Eyes of an Ass 19
6. Paul and the Signs of the Zodiac 22
7. The Monotony of Security 25
8. Is Gay Really Groovey? 28
9. Too Young to Die? 31
10. Incurably Religious 34
11. To Serve or Not to Serve? 37
12. Would You Name Your Son Judas? 40
13. Does God Change His Mind? 43
14. Be Careful . . . God May Be Looking 46
15. More Hope for a Fool 49
16. To Quibble or Not to Quibble 52
17. Yes, the Fat Is in Your Head 55
18. Blessed Be Nothing 58
19. Blessing and Curse of the Quill 61
20. What More? 64
21. Out of Wine? 67
22. A Radical Book? 70
23. How to Be Wiser Than Your Teachers 73
24. What's in Your Soul-Winner's Kit? 76
25. Listen, Stonehead! 79
26. How to Kill a Missionary 82
27. Prayers Minus Piety Equals Nothing 85
28. Do You Know the Author's Name? 88
29. A Real Experience 91
30. The Great Commission or the Great Confusion? 94

1
SOME PORK CHOPS, PETER?

WHAT IF . . .

"Oh boy, do I need a vacation!"

Who but God would tell a zealous Jew to kill a pig, prepare some pork chops, and eat them? And who among the early believers but Peter would look God in the face and say, "Not me, Lord"?

Interesting, isn't it, the length God will go to to teach basic lessons to His children. Peter's problem, like a lot of the rest of us, was that he did not know God loves people. Of course, Peter would have been the first to confess that God loved Peter's little circle of people. But for God to love the world—the Gentile world—that was impossible. Weren't the Gentiles dogs? And surely Peter had not been chosen by the Saviour to share the love of God with animals.

And that is the very reason the sheet Peter saw that day in Joppa was filled with animals. God was telling Peter that there is no one He cannot make clean.

Though some people are as covetous as vultures and others as cruel as leopards, God can cleanse them. Though some may be as stubborn as mules or as sly as the fox, God can change them. Though some may wallow in the slime of immorality while others are wolves in sheep's clothing, they are not beyond the life-transforming power of the Gospel. Though the mouths of some are filled with the poison of the cobra and the hearts of others filled with evil continually, there is a message that will change their lives.

Yes, God loves people, all kinds of people. Not just the weak little lamb who is so ready to respond, but also that *dog*—that mean, barking dog who makes so much noise about his cynicism, agnosticism, or atheism. That *pig* who is so mired down in alcoholism, sex, or dope. That *skunk* whose deceitful dealings with widows and orphans smell to high heaven. That proud *peacock* who struts around in colorful religious attire because he wants to be seen and heard of men.

I used to criticize you, Peter, for being so stupid— for allowing your religious bigotry to blind you to God's love for people. But not anymore. I think it might do me a lot of good if God would let down a sheet full of Hindus and Muslims, Buddhists and Shintoists, animists and devil worshipers before me. Or should a map and a few statistics do it for me?

Paul did not have to have a sheet let down from heaven to convince him that God loves people. He was, therefore, ready to eat meat or give up eating meat if it would increase his opportunities to win men to Christ. Thanks, Paul. You were ahead of most of the believers of your day. And perhaps of mine.

2
JOSEPH AND SITUATION ETHICS

WHAT IF . . .

"It's OK, Joseph. Potiphar and I have an open marriage."

Put together a beautiful bedroom, a scantily clad, sexually hungry woman, and a handsome young servant and you have the basic ingredients for an exciting experience in situation ethics. You will find the whole picture in Genesis 39, not in *Playboy*.

The wife of Egypt's chief executioner had spent many days feeding her passions for her good-looking, Jewish slave. This gave young Joseph the opportunity to evaluate the pros and cons of his responsibility. He had served well in Potiphar's household. He had obeyed every order and responded to every whim of his master. As a result, the running of the household and the supervision of other slaves had fallen to him. The keys of the house were his to turn.

Potiphar's wife timed her actions well. Her husband had gone to the palace and would not be back for the day. The other servants were well occupied outside the house.

"Joseph, come here immediately."
"Yes, Ma'am. Where are you?"
"I am in the bedroom. I need you."
"Yes, Ma'am."
"Joseph, lie with me."

And why shouldn't he? Wasn't it a slave's responsibility to be obedient to the one who owned him? Didn't her passion for him prove that her deepest physical longings were not being satisfied by her husband? If he could give her a few minutes of pleasure, why should he refuse? Couldn't he make this an expression of *love?* And could he be sure his head would not roll if he dared to disobey her?

For Potiphar's wife the situation was perfect. There were no moral standards in her heart or home to keep her from sleeping with Joseph if she desired it. The house was her kingdom, and it was her right to order her slaves to fulfill her every desire.

But Joseph had never heard of situation ethics. He had learned to walk in the light of God's character. There was no situation that would make adultery right for him. The options were crystal clear. He could obey this tempting display of feminine flesh, and sin against God. Or, he could obey God and suffer the consequences. He could yield to the throbbing desires of her flesh and of his, or he could run from them.

Joseph did not waste time making up his mind. His reaction was one of instant recoil. He made a hasty retreat into genuine victory. Somehow, somewhere, or from someone, he had learned that it costs far more to disobey God than to obey Him.

Thanks, Joseph, for reminding the rest of us.

3
WATCH OUT! SOMEBODY LOVES YOU!

WHAT IF . . .

"Has it ever occurred to you that you lack a sense of personal worth?"

"I hate myself; and if you knew me like I know me, you would hate me like I hate me." His voice is filled with bitterness toward himself in particular and the world in general. And like a lot of other teen-age self-haters, he is deliberately committing a slow form of suicide through a surrender to alcohol, nicotine, sex, and dope.

He is not a prodigal son running away from a good home. He never had one. He has no concept of what it would mean to leave the barnyard in which he is feeding on the moral slop that is thrown to the pigs and return to a loving father. He has never had a loving father. The tragedy is—there are millions like him in our world today. They seem to be screaming to a deaf world, "Won't somebody love me?"

But not all self-haters come from that kind of background. Many people who have been raised in good surroundings have never learned to accept themselves. They have never been able to say honestly, "I love me." Of course, some have been able to put on a facade of self-respect. Some have even been able to hide their self-disdain behind a tall image of proud self-importance. But behind it all they are being eaten up with a strong sense of worthlessness.

There is, of course, no place for self-disdain in the life of the fellow or girl, man or woman who has faith in Jesus Christ. Room to hate my sin? Surely! Room to hate myself? Never!

If you are troubled about this self-acceptance bit, swing into the following routine of spiritual gymnastics. Start each day thanking God:

1. For creating you for Himself. He made you the way you are in order that He might glorify His name through you in a way distinctive from that by which He brings glory to Himself through anyone else.

2. For considering you worth redeeming. Your purchase price was pretty high, and He must have

loved you a great deal to pay it.

3. For placing you in Christ. That's right! You are accepted "in the Beloved." That is certainly a worth-holding-your-head-up place to be.

4. For making your body His home. Doesn't He say your body is the temple of the Holy Spirit? That should be really meaningful to you.

5. For promising you that He will complete the good work He has begun in you. God is not through with you yet. When He is, you will be proud of the results.

Yes, Somebody loves you, and absorbing all His love for you would be like trying to drink all the water of all the rivers of all the world.

4
THAT PROBLEM OF PRIORITIES

WHAT IF . . .

"Tell Jesus I'll be along at halftime."

"You have time to do anything you want to do." That is what the preacher shot at me, and it was a bull's-eye. That very afternoon I had spent three hours watching a professional football game on television. There were, of course, several things of more importance I should have been doing; but I did not do them. I did the thing I wanted to do. It was all a matter of priorities.

This priority bit has been a battle for me in the field of prayer and Bible study for years. I have continually found myself wanting to do other things at the expense of those two essentials to my Christian growth. My difficulty has not really been one of time but of desire. And I suppose desires, like appetites, have to be developed.

I did not start my Christian life with a full-blown appetite for either prayer or Bible study. I began as a newborn babe, desiring the sincere milk of God's Word, and developed a good appetite for the meat of the Word. But even after a healthy taste for fellowship with God has been developed, it has to be persistently guarded in the face of the goodies offered by the world, the flesh, and the devil. And there's the rub.

What in the world can I do to assure myself that I will once and forever put first things first? Nothing! In fact, I am making a mistake in even seeking such a panacea. The price of proper priorities is eternal vigilance. The Lord expressed it in this manner: just keep seeking the kingdom of God first. And that cuts across the grain of my nature. It is normal for me to seek *my* kingdom first.

So, what do I do? I keep on keeping on in prayer and Bible study. When I foul up my priorities, I ask His forgiveness. When I am successful in keeping them straight, I thank Him for the strength He is giving me to do it.

I guess it ultimately boils down to "lovest thou Me more than these?" And I am thankful that love is a two-party involvement in which the Other Party is more interested in my love for Him than I am.

I am glad He will go on doing everything He can to keep drawing my love in His direction. My faith rests in the fact that God is working in me, helping me want to obey Him, and then helping me do what He wants (see Phil. 2:13).

5
OH, FOR THE EYES OF AN ASS

WHAT IF . . .

"Now that you mention it, Balaam, the king's reward **would** buy a lot of oats."

I do not know whether all asses have eyes that are able to bring angels into focus or not, but I do know that we humans are pretty blind to them. It makes me wonder how many times angels have tried to stop me in some of my detours out of the will of God only to discover that I failed to recognize them and went blindly on my way. Balaam was certainly not the first or last man who has been blind to the guidance of the Lord.

I can easily picture Balaam's ass pulling against the reins as he wanders off the road and into a field. I can almost feel the lash of Balaam's whip on the poor animal's back. I can hear Balaam's cry of pain as the frightened beast crushes his rider's foot against a stone wall. I can easily imagine Balaam's anger as his ass falls to the ground to avoid going closer to the sword-swinging angel. I can see Balaam and his two servants beating, kicking, and cursing the beast.

Then all at once the braying ass becomes a praying creature. "What have I done? Haven't I served you well? Why are you beating me? Can't you see that there is a reason back of the things that are happening to you?" (see Num. 22)

The *blind* obedience of Balaam's ass, of the frogs in Egypt, of the succulent quail in the wilderness, of Elijah's raven, and of the fish that filled the disciples' net in Galilee excites my imagination. The *blind* disobedience of those of us who are believers amazes me. Of course, like Balaam, we rationalize our willfulness and compromise our commitment. A bit more money, a little more comfort, or success, or popularity, or a dozen other things have subtle ways of diverting us from God's will.

King Saul could not see that the things that were happening to him were forewarnings of his downfall. Samson was blind to the fact that each time he rested his head on Delilah's lap he was moving closer to his own destruction. Joshua did not realize that God was trying to say something to Israel through the defeat at Ai.

I wonder what we would see if we had eyes to bring angels into focus. Would we see God trying to say something to us through the loss of a job, sickness, an automobile accident, or some other difficulty? I cannot answer those questions, but I am thankful that the death of Balaam's ass did not bring to an end God's desire to keep men from going astray even though He sometimes has to use drastic measures.

6
PAUL AND SIGNS OF THE ZODIAC

WHAT IF . . .

"Let's see, you were born in Tarsus under the sign of Cancer. I see a name change in your future."

The occult is growing. Palmists, false prophets, and soothsayers are multiplying. The syndicated columns of astrologers are being assiduously studied by increasing millions of people. All of this seems to suggest that times of uncertainty tend to arouse man's longing to know the future—or at least his future. It also suggests that the Church needs to give men a solid foundation on which to stand.

It can be said without fear of contradiction that all the astrologers of the past 2,000 years have not so benefited mankind as the little man whose name was long ago changed from Saul to Paul. And no astrologer had ever predicted that would happen.

Though the mystery and miracle of Saul's conversion from a Christ-hating Pharisee to the most indomitable, dynamic warrior of the Cross in all of Christian history has often been debated, it cannot be explained apart from a genuine work of God. No sign of Cancer, sunstrokes, or psychological experience can account for the personal transformation and the persistent, long-suffering, total dedication of this man to the will and work of God.

Paul tells about his life-changing and name-changing conversion in the simplest of words. He was on his way to Damascus armed with the authority and filled with the determination to persecute followers of the Way unto death. Then all at once he was stopped by a blinding light, and he heard a voice saying, "Saul, Saul, why are you persecuting Me?"

His response was, "Who are you, Lord?"

The answer: "I am Jesus of Nazareth, whom thou persecutest" (see Acts 22:4-8).

A few days later, a Christian believer said to Saul, "The God of our fathers has appointed you to know His will, and to see the Righteous One, and to hear an utterance from His mouth. For you will be a witness for Him to all men of what you have seen and heard" (Acts 22:14, *New American Standard Bible*).

Paul describes all of this as a "heavenly vision"

to which he was immediately obedient. The price of that obedience included repeated imprisonment, being beaten with rods, lashed five times with 39 stripes, being stoned, being shipwrecked, and finally being placed in a dark Roman cell to await death. Through it all Paul was zealous and faithful. He had become a new creature in Christ, and he demonstrated his gratitude to God by living and dying for Him.

Anyone tempted to question the conversion of this man who became Paul can do no better than to read his writings. His epistles (letters) tell a great deal about the depth of his faith in Jesus Christ. Better yet, they tell a great deal about Jesus Christ. In fact, one cannot understand Paul apart from Jesus Christ. And our understanding of Christ would also be greatly circumscribed without Paul.

7
THE MONOTONY OF SECURITY

WHAT IF . . .

"He looks terrible after 40 days in the wilderness. I don't think God meant for anyone to ruin his health."

"I know You are hungry, but I also know a practical answer to Your need. Just turn one or two of these stones into bread. It is hardly fitting for You to leave this wilderness looking like You have been fasting." Those suggestions of the Evil One were not

25

without some content of truth. In fact, the father of lies seldom speaks without inserting truth into what he says. What better way to deceive people?

Christ's answer to that subtle temptation was a quote from the Old Testament, "Man shall not live by bread alone" (Deut. 8:3; Matt. 4:4). It points an accusing finger at a world of men and women who are caught in the vortex of materialism. It cuts across the grain of that philosophy which says, "Eat, drink, and be merry, for tomorrow we die." It judges the man who puts his belly ahead of his soul and time ahead of eternity.

To the believer in Christ who feels that God "certainly wants me to protect my health," it gives room for serious thought. To protect one's health for Jesus' sake or to live comfortably because the servant of the Lord deserves the best is often a rationalizing of one's desire to escape the discipline of sacrificial living.

There is nothing in the life of Him who had no bed He could call His own to suggest that comfort or material benefits are essential to effective service. In fact, the very opposite seems to be true.

Though discipline, sacrifice, and frugality are not necessarily the keys to spiritual power, the lack of them often short-circuits one's usefulness to God. Easy-chair Christianity does not contribute to the conquering of continents for Christ.

There was nothing in the life of Paul and many others in the Early Church to indicate they placed any great amount of value on financial well-being or physical safety. They counted not their lives dear unto themselves in order to win men to Christ. Concern about the homes in which they lived, the clothes they wore, the vehicles they drove, or the food they ate consumed little of their interest. They were in a war, and battles are not won by men entangled with things. Exploits are not accomplished by people who are at ease in Zion.

Christ's long, hard 40 days of prayer in the wilderness makes my four minutes a day seem woefully inadequate. His fasting rebukes my gluttony. His clothes look inexpensive, His bed hard, and His food commonplace compared to mine. He knew nothing of the monotony of security. He lived in the excitement of daily sacrificing His time and strength to the accomplishing of God's will. Perhaps we have a lot to learn about walking in His footsteps.

8
IS GAY REALLY GROOVY?

WHAT IF . . .

"You fellows don't seem to understand—my calling is to bless, support, and sustain the folks of Sodom in their homosexual lives."

It was an amazing discovery. I mean that one the president's commission on pornography came up with a few years ago. The majority opinion of the commission was that a man can drink out of all the sewers and eat from all the garbage cans he desires and not get sick. I refer, of course, to the sewers and garbage cans of immorality. Fortunately, medical science has not stooped to the level of dishing out that kind of dirty advice to those who want to stay physically healthy.

If there is one thing that speaks more loudly than another about the depravity of human nature, it is the pronouncements of educated men who decry moral standards. I have a hunch they are defending their own lack of them. Of course, there are 101 other demonstrations of human depravity, not the least of which is our mass media. Our newspapers give us all the sordid details of man's sin. Our radios talk and sing about it, and our television programs picture it in all the forms of greed, hate, lust, war, and murder that can be imagined.

But the mass media can reveal no crime so heinous that it will surprise the man who is an honest student of his own heart. Nor will it surprise the man who makes it a habit to study his Bible. In the Word of God he sees the lust, vile imaginations, and viciousness of man. He hears Jeremiah say, "The heart is deceitful above all things and desperately wicked" (17:9). He reads Christ's statement, "For out of the heart proceed evil thoughts, murders, adulteries, fornications, thefts, false witness, blasphemies" (Matt. 15:19).

To all of this is added the testimony of the first three chapters of Romans. In them he discovers that "there is none righteous, no, not one. All have sinned, and come short of the glory of God" (Rom. 3:10, 23). Even while knowing right from wrong, men choose evil. They love darkness rather than light. And with all of this, a Christian's own heart bears testimony, for he knows he is just a sinner saved by God's grace.

The Christian reads of the horrible homosexuality of Sodom and Gomorrah (Gen. 18—19) and does not find the vile wickedness of those cities hard to believe. He studies God's pronouncements of judgment against those who pervert sex and who change love to lust. He finds it difficult to understand how any Christian denomination could look upon homosexuality as anything less than the perverting, defiling, and damning vile affection that it is (Rom. 1:26-27). He knows that gay is not groovy. He is prepared to share the message of God's grace with the homosexual or any other sinner, but he is not prepared to condone his sin.

9
TOO YOUNG TO DIE?

WHAT IF . . .

"Pastor, I've just never been able to get over the fear of dying young!"

Would you really rather be on earth or in heaven? If you prefer heaven, why? Are you just sick of it all here? If so, your motive for moving is not very exalted.

If you prefer to be here, what are your motives? Are they related to things you still want to see and do? Or do you have family and business responsibilities no one else can quite take over? Or are you still in the prime of life—just too young to die?

King Hezekiah of the Old Testament pled with God for more time on earth. At 39 years of age he was told to put his house in order for his time to die had arrived. He could not believe it. After all, look what he had accomplished. Sweeping religious reform and spiritual revival had followed in the wake of his leadership in Judah. Fourteen years of glorious progress and prosperity had accompanied the reign of this king who was so deeply committed to God.

Hezekiah doubtless rationalized his desire to spend more time on earth. He was too young to die; he had plans he wanted to see fulfilled; and he was not sure about the grave. Perhaps such ideas ring a bell with a lot of us who ought to know better.

God never calls unto Himself any of His own who are too young to die. His Son (crucified in His early 30s) was not too young to die. John the Baptist (beheaded in his 30s) was not too young to die. Brainerd at 29, Borden of Yale, and the five Auca martyrs, all young men, were not too young to die. There are no premature deaths among God's children.

Only the heavenly Father knows when the work He has given us is finished. Our work may not appear complete to us or even to the friends who are watching us; but God sees the whole picture. He considers what He is finishing in us as well as what we are finishing for Him. Furthermore, He knows the potential tragedies He will save us from by taking us home in His time. No child of God has ever lived on earth too short a time.

Then again, God fully knows the glories of heaven and the sacredness of service to which He calls His own there. Should we who believe that to be with Christ is far better ever seriously feel that any Christian is too young to die? And who isn't young in the light of eternity? Whether it is your three score years and ten or Methuselah's 969 years, all believers die young. And how does one compare a few score years with eternity, anyway?

The issue is not length of years on earth but the quality of life lived. In the light of this, we need not be overly concerned about 15 more years or even one more year. Our concern should be that at the close of any day we are prepared to say to God, as Jesus did, "I have glorified Thee on the earth; I have finished the work which Thou gavest Me to do" (John 17:4).

10
INCURABLY RELIGIOUS

WHAT IF . . .

"Men of Athens, we have come not to impose new religious concepts on you but to hear your insights into the unknown god."

Hinduism promotes the worship of the monkey god, the elephant-headed god, and 30 million other gods. I suppose Hindus added many gods to their list for fear they might miss some deity and thus arouse his displeasure. Like the religious Athenians, who centuries ago erected an altar "To the unknown god," Hinduism's many idols add testimony to the fact that people are incurably religious. All men, even atheists, seem to have a few unknown gods in their lives. Some of those gods are not put on display except in times of crisis.

Paul did not waste any time *dialoguing* with the Athenians as to what characteristics the unknown god might have, or as to the benefits he was expected to confer on those who worshiped him. He saw in the altar of the unknown god a platform from which to proclaim Christ. In this he teaches us some great lessons.

Paul does not berate his listeners (Gentile idol worshipers) for being religious. He uses it as a stepping-stone to lead them from whatever light they had to greater light. And this suggests that though it is profitable to know the basics of another man's religious beliefs, we are not apt to win him to the Saviour if we beat him over the head with the errors we find in his religion.

It was completely impossible for Paul to synchronize his faith in a resurrected Saviour with the worship of idols. His listeners recognized this, and some of them mocked him when he talked about Christ being raised from the dead. He was, nevertheless, adamant unto death in his conviction that Jesus was the one and only way to God. Any other gospel was no gospel at all to Paul.

In this day of religious permissiveness, it is amazingly easy to compromise one's faith in the Cross. It is easy to forget that "biblical faith is unique because it is revealed." According to the Word of God, Jesus Christ is God's final and complete message to man. To add to or change that fact is to pervert it.

Christianity is, therefore, not a comparative religion any more than Jesus Christ is a comparative religious leader. You do not compare God with man. You contrast them, just as you contrast light and darkness or life and death.

No other name than Jesus has been given to men, says the Bible, whereby they can be saved (see Acts 4:12). Gautama, Mohammad, and Confucius may be great names in the religious field, but they are not worthy to be compared to the name of Jesus Christ. They are of the earth, earthy. He is the eternal, self-existent One.

If the implacably unreligious or the incurably religious are ever to enter heaven, it will be through Christ. When men exchange their unknown gods for a relationship with Him, whom to know is life eternal, they enter into the joy of salvation.

11
TO SERVE OR NOT TO SERVE?

WHAT IF . . .

"My call to the priesthood? I remember it well. I was sitting there leafing through **Playboy** magazine . . . ."

Yes, they actually did it! A well-known religious organization placed an ad in America's best known pornographic rag inviting men interested in joining the clergy to respond. They got some response, and that is not too surprising. Most men are ready for anything that might offer prestige or suggest economic advance.

At any rate, the Bible is consistent in placing one's call to the ministry on a very high level. There is nothing *Playboy* about it.

Moses' life of service for God grew out of some face-to-face verbal sparring in which God backed Moses into a corner and then answered every objection he had. From that day on, Moses' voice rang with a "thus-saith-the-Lord" note of authority. His ability to shake his fist in Pharaoh's face, to order Israel to cross the Red Sea, to stand true to God in the midst of much complaining and backsliding during 40 long years in the wilderness grew out of his unshakable conviction that he was God's man. There was withstandability in his work for God.

And how does one account for the years of godly life and leadership seen in such men as Joseph, Joshua, and Daniel? Could any one of them have lived in the moral and spiritual morass which surrounded him apart from an unshakable assurance that God Himself had placed His hand upon him?

Isaiah's separation unto the service of God is well known (Isa. 6). God, the high and holy One, appeared to him in a vision he was never able to forget. That sanctifying experience became the soil out of which Isaiah's long and fruitful ministry grew.

Jeremiah was told, "Before I formed thee in the belly I knew thee; and before thou camest forth out of the womb I sanctified thee, and I ordained thee a prophet unto the nations" (Jer. 1:5). It is little wonder that this prophet with a tender heart stood true to God in the dungeon and in captivity.

And how does one explain Paul and countless other men and women who have walked in his footsteps? They were God-ordained, God-sent, God-empowered, and God-kept—*and they knew it!* This enabled them to enter into battle and to win. Withstandability and fruitfulness come only to that child of God who knows he is a God-chosen vessel.

12
WOULD YOU NAME YOUR SON JUDAS?

WHAT IF . . .

"Forget the money, Judas! Any guy who can turn water into wine is the kind of front man our revolution needs."

Of all the ways to get one's name into history, none could have been more despicable than selling history's greatest Man for 30 pieces of silver. Of course, Judas was not trying to get his name in history. He was a self-deceived, devil-deluded individual who felt that if Jesus would not overthrow the enslaving Roman Empire, He deserved to be betrayed.

Though I am not prepared to defend the pathetic *son of perdition* who betrayed Jesus, I think there may be more of the spirit of Judas in most of us than we are ready to admit.

There seem to be millions of people who deliberately barter the will of God for passing pleasures worth far less than 30 pieces of silver. They have betrayed the love of God and sold their own souls for a bank account, a higher salary, a better home, a nice car, a color television, a Sunday of pleasure, a night of lust, a bottle of whiskey, or even a reefer. They serve the devil for peanuts.

Sadly, the betrayal of one's own eternal welfare is not left to the godless. Many followers of Christ prove by their actions that they are not entirely free from the spirit of Judas.

What is it that allows a believer to give "30 pieces of silver" to the work of world evangelization while spending $9,000 on a car or $65,000 on a new home? What, but the spirit of Judas!

What is it that enables Christians to give 30 days a month to their jobs, homes, clubs, and social activities, but keeps them from giving three days a month to the church and soul-winning? What, but the spirit of Judas!

Why do we sing heartily, "Give of thy sons to bear the message glorious; give of thy wealth to speed them on their way," only to hold back both sons and silver from the service of the Saviour? Isn't this the spirit of Judas?

What is it that enables Christians to rise up early for golf games and fishing trips, and yet provides no ambition to spend an early hour interceding for the souls of lost men and women? What, but the spirit of Judas!

Of course, Christians would not name their sons, Judas, but do their sons see more of his characteristics in their parents than one might expect?

We seem to be of those who can say, "We are rich and increased with goods, and have need of nothing," while in the perspective of the betrayed and risen Christ, we are poor, wretched, miserable, and blind (see Rev. 3:17). Maybe our slavery to materialism is more idolatrous and dangerous than we realized. Maybe there is a bit more of the spirit of Judas in us than we are prepared to admit. Then, may God help us.

13
DOES GOD CHANGE HIS MIND?

WHAT IF . . .

"Since my 'Thus saith the Lord' of last week, several things have happened, and the Lord has changed His mind."

Mr. Jones changed his mind because of days of Communist brainwashing. Or perhaps it is fairer to Mr. Jones to say he had his mind changed for him by unbearable pressure.

Television ads changed Mrs. Smith's mind. She had repeatedly said she would never use Brightudent toothpaste, but she is using it.

It was political advantage that changed Mr. Arnold's mind. He could obtain more votes by reversing his position on the ecology issue.

John Brown did not take long to change his mind when he was told of the economic gain that would be his by going on strike or slowing production on a crucial energy product.

Love changed Beth Anderson's mind. For years she had studied and worked toward becoming a doctor. Then Cupid came along, and now she is a wife and mother.

A progression of truth changed the mind of the unnamed Samaritan woman in John 4. She saw Jesus first as just a Jewish stranger, then as a prophet, and finally as the Messiah.

A miracle experience changed the mind of the blind man of John 9. He had never heard of a man born blind being healed. Nor did he have a mind to believe anyone could do it until he met Jesus. But after that experience, all the threatening of the Pharisees could not alter his faith.

Conversion changed the mind of Paul. He who had breathed out threatenings and slaughter against believers in Christ all at once became their strongest protagonist.

And whether we speak of Thomas or Peter, the Samaritan women, the blind man, or Paul, it could be said that increased information and the convicting power of the Holy Spirit changed their minds.

But who is there to give God added information or new ideas? What pressures can be brought against Him? What political advantages or economic gains await Him? It is not conceivable that the omniscient One ever has to change His mind. His "thus saith the Lord" is exactly that.

Then how about God's dealings with Nineveh? Didn't He tell Jonah He would destroy Nineveh in 40 days? And didn't He then spare the city? Exactly! Then, didn't He change His mind? Not at all! It has always been the mind of God to punish sin. It has also always been His mind to show mercy to the repentant. These unalterable facts are a part of the character of God. Even Jonah knew that (Jonah 4:2-3).

14
BE CAREFUL... GOD MAY BE LOOKING

WHAT IF . . .

"Ananias, you say your previous statement is now 'inoperative'?"

The only serious sin is that of getting caught. At least, that seems to be the moral philosophy of millions of us. And, like the thief, we do not expect to get caught. So, we keep on deceiving, cheating, stealing, lusting, hating, blaspheming, even murdering.

When will we learn that the man who sins is already caught? He is a servant of the evil, unkind, or unjust thing he does. Or when will we learn that sin has a way of finding us out—a way of pointing the finger at us? It has its own built-in consequences, some of which etch themselves into our characters or on our faces.

Then what about this idea that God is watching? The Bible clearly expresses it in these words, "Thou God seest me."

You do not like the idea? Well, I suppose the child who refrains from doing something naughty because Mom or Dad is watching does not like the idea, either. But maybe that child will live long enough to thank God his parents cared enough to stop him from doing wrong things by keeping their eyes on him.

Perhaps you remember the story of the Israelite soldier who hid some of the spoils of Jericho in his tent (Josh. 7). His shrewd thinking and skillful maneuvering enabled him to complete the job without being seen by anyone. That is, anyone but God. He paid an awful price for trying to do something behind God's back.

King David was confident he had done a rather clever job of hiding his adultery from all observers. But just to make sure, he had the witness who could really point the finger at him put to death. Then about the time David began to feel he had done a good cover-up job, Nathan stepped in and lifted the lid. God had seen the whole, sordid mess.

Apart from a direct revelation to Peter by the Holy Spirit, the sin of Ananias and his wife, Sapphira, would have never been known to the Church. But God was watching and for their sake, for the Church's sake, and for His own sake, He could not allow their deceitfulness to continue. Whom did Ananias really think he was fooling?

Maybe it is good for us to know God is watching —watching not only when we are tempted to do wrong, but watching with pleasure when we do right.

phira, would have never been known to the Church. But God was watching and for their sake, for the Church's sake, and for His own sake, He could not allow their deceitfulness to continue. Whom did Ananias really think he was fooling?

Maybe it is good for us to know God is watching —watching not only when we are tempted to do wrong, but watching with pleasure when we do right.

to get caught. So, we keep on deceiving, cheating, stealing, lusting, hating, blaspheming, even murdering.

When will we learn that the man who sins is already caught? He is a servant of the evil, unkind, or unjust thing he does. Or when will we learn that sin has a way of finding us out—a way of pointing the finger at us? It has its own built-in consequences, some of which etch themselves into our characters or on our faces.

Then what about this idea that God is watching? The Bible clearly expresses it in these words, "Thou God seest me."

You do not like the idea? Well, I suppose the child who refrains from doing something naughty because Mom or Dad is watching does not like the idea, either. But maybe that child will live long enough to thank God his parents cared enough to stop him from doing wrong things by keeping their eyes on him.

Perhaps you remember the story of the Israelite soldier who hid some of the spoils of Jericho in his tent (Josh. 7). His shrewd thinking and skillful maneuvering enabled him to complete the job without being seen by anyone. That is, anyone but God. He paid an awful price for trying to do something behind God's back.

King David was confident he had done a rather clever job of hiding his adultery from all observers. But just to make sure, he had the witness who could really point the finger at him put to death. Then about the time David began to feel he had done a good cover-up job, Nathan stepped in and lifted the lid. God had seen the whole, sordid mess.

Apart from a direct revelation to Peter by the Holy Spirit, the sin of Ananias and his wife, Sap-

15
MORE HOPE FOR A FOOL

WHAT IF . . .

"His head on a platter? What are you, some kind of a nut?"

Herod the Edomite blew it. He watched a scantily clad teen-ager do a dance that aroused all his masculine corpuscles. Then, in the heat of unthinking passion, he called her close to his side and promised her anything she wanted.

It is amazing how passion can rob a man of his senses. It would be difficult to imagine a sovereign making a more rash promise to a young lady than the one Herod made that day. But Herod was neither the first nor the last man to be hasty with words and then live to regret it. Samson, Jephthah, Saul, David, and Peter are but a few of the Bible characters who spoke rashly or made ludicrous statements in the heat of emotional experiences. There is more hope for a fool than for a man who spouts off at the mouth, says Solomon.

But watch with me for a minute as Herod's wife sits up in bed and stares wide-eyed at the door. Listen as she screams, "Take it away. Somebody please take that platter away from me. That head! Those eyes! They are driving me crazy!"

Then hear Herod's response, "Shut up and go to sleep. You are just having a nightmare. If you weren't so stupid, you wouldn't have had your daughter ask me to behead John the Baptist. Why in the world did I listen to her, anyway?"

Yes, Herod, why did you listen?

You listened because you did not have the strength to admit you had made a horrible mistake in promising half your kingdom to your stepdaughter. Only strong men admit their mistakes. Only men with character say, "I'm sorry." Only men with courage confess their sins. And, Herod, you are not that kind of a man. You are more concerned about what people think of you than about what God thinks. Expediency is more important to you than principle, even though it means shedding the blood of the best friend you could have ever had. Now you will have to go on living with your guilt-laden conscience, with your hysterical and illicit wife, and your frustrated step-daughter.

Your experience, Herod, has something to say to those of us who live in the 20th century. Something about the necessity of guarding the words of our mouths, about not being rash with our promises, and about being big enough, strong enough, courageous enough, and Christian enough to confess our mistakes before it is too late.

16
TO QUIBBLE OR NOT TO QUIBBLE

WHAT IF . . .

"Did you have in mind the Jebusite cubit, the Hivite cubit, or the Canaanite cubit?"

It is apocryphal, but good. It seems a certain survivor of the Jamestown flood insisted on telling his story wherever he went. He even insisted on telling it in heaven. Just before he began his account, Gabriel leaned over to him and whispered, "Sir, I think you should know, Noah is in the audience."

I suppose Noah has a greater story to tell than we have ever realized. What an epoch his very name suggests.

The bigger the job God gives a man, the easier it is to find excuses for not doing it. Given Noah's job, my excuses would probably sound like this:

But, Lord, I am not sure I understand what you want.

But, Lord, it has never been done before!

But, Lord, I'm not the one to do it. I don't even know how to saw a straight line.

But, Lord, it is too big a job. I will never get it done.

But, Lord, where will I get all the lumber?

But, Lord, people will think I am crazy.

But, Lord, no one has ever heard of a flood.

But, Lord, it won't be possible to get those animals into the ark.

But, Lord, how do I know it will float when it is loaded?

But, Lord, don't You know what that place will smell like after a few days? And anyway, I do have a few plans of my own.

All those excuses (and that is what they are) fail to recognize two simple facts: (1) God knows how big the assignment is, and (2) He knows who the man is He wants to fulfill that assignment. In other words, He does not choose me for a job without knowing He can complete it through me.

I am glad Noah was asked to do the job. His amazing step of faith is a straight-to-the-jaw rebuke to my unbelief. He built an ark for the saving of his household. And that tells me that we can never quite know just how far-reaching the blessings of our obedience might be.

Apparently, Noah was not a nit-picker. He did not waste any time arguing with God about the details of his assignment. He had an ark to build, and he got right to it. Over 100 years later, he finished the job. Perhaps that has a lesson for us. Perhaps we would get more building done in the church if we quibbled less about details. Like Noah's household, your family and mine will only be saved if they get into the ark of God's love. It is a big assignment. Let's get on with it.

17
YES, THE FAT IS IN YOUR HEAD

WHAT IF . . .

"Be healed of obesity!"

It was about 3,000 years ago that Solomon said *the fat is in your head*. In fact, he made it stronger than that. He said, the wise man will put a knife to his throat rather than eat too much (see Prov. 23:2).

Though spoken in a context other than obesity, this graphic expression surely indicates that severe action sometimes has to be taken if we are going to accomplish some of the things that need to be done. One who was far wiser than Solomon said something similar when He declared that if your eye is going to be the instrument that sends you to hell, you'd better have it taken out.

The obvious principle behind this is that when there is something wrong, we have an obligation to help make it right. If our eyes are reading magazines or books they shouldn't or watching television programs they shouldn't, we are not to ask God to burn the books or turn off the television. He will not do it. But He will give us the strength to do it.

We are not to ask God to take the ice cream and cake from the table. We are to ask Him to help us close our mouths so tightly we cannot get a spoon between our teeth.

There is a fine line between resting in what God has done or will do for us and in that which we must do for ourselves. Faith and obedience are Siamese twins.

It is one thing to say, "I am crucified with Christ." It is another to put to death the deeds of the flesh. To walk according to the desires of the flesh is both normal and fatal. To walk in the Spirit is a miracle experienced only by those who prayerfully discipline themselves in it. It is learned by dependent and persistent effort. No man drifts into a victorious life.

Paul speaks about striving for the mastery, fighting to win, and bringing his body into subjection (1 Cor. 9:24-27). Whether our deepest problems are rooted in the lusts of the flesh, the desires of the eyes, or the pride of life, we are to put the knife to them.

Meg Woodson tells of praying for deliverance

from cream puffs and chocolate eclairs only to become "a 210-pound zero." Then she made a vow to God that she would never again take another bite of cake, candy, pudding, or pie. She found she had to strive to keep her vow; and in the very act of doing so, she experienced the quickening power of the Spirit. "I am convinced," she says, "that the more rational, determined, pervasive effort a Christian makes to live the Christian life, the more fully the grace of God is able to operate within."

The Bible says, "faith without works is dead" (James 2:20). And whether we relate it to the problem of losing weight or winning souls, it seems to be an immutable principle.

18
BLESSED BE NOTHING

WHAT IF . . .

"It's not that I mind leaving Ur, but I've got an 800 shekel mortgage on this tent in a depressed market."

Tenting became a familiar experience to me during my days as a missionary in India. Every "cold season" (hyperbole), my wife and I would spend two or three months moving our tent from village to village as we shared the love of God with people throughout the district. Of course, I was not in the land of my inheritance, nor was I dwelling in tabernacles with Isaac and Jacob. But I was learning a few important and instructive lessons about tenting.

The first lesson is suggested by the word *availability*. Tents are not provided with a comfortable, second-story bedroom in which to hide away. If you cough or snore, even at midnight, people know you are there. And, more often than not, those outside the tent are happy to let you know they are waiting outside for help of some kind or another.

But then, isn't availability what the Christian life is all about? Isn't it about the most significant ability God desires of us? Isn't it the ability lonely people need to see in us most?

Frugality was the second lesson that tenting taught me. There was no space in our tent for most of the things modern man looks upon as necessities. Even if there had been space, most of those things would have been horribly out of place. We were living among believers whose greatest luxury was the anticipation of someday dwelling in that eternal city whose builder and maker is God (Heb. 11:10).

I discovered frugality is a blessed virtue. It has the happy faculty of weaning a man away from the idolatry of materialism. It contributes much to the heart of anyone who really wants to set his affections on things above.

Mobility describes the third lesson I learned in the tent. It would be an expensive and rather cumbersome job to raise a $50,000 house and move it any distance. Add to that the two-car garage and the swimming pool and your problems are multiplied. About that time, immobility begins to look more practical and sound more harmonious.

But how does one delete mobility from Christian experience? If we are pilgrims and strangers here on earth, what right do we have to dig our foundations so deep we become immobile?

The very bodies we live in are really only tents. Perhaps, then, we should be somewhat less concerned about the things with which we surround them. Perhaps availability, frugality, and mobility should play a larger part in the lives of those of us who claim citizenship in heaven.

19
THE BLESSING OF THE QUILL

WHAT IF . . .

"In a hundred years, Martin, no one will remember your little tiff with the Pope."

Thanks to Henry Ford, the world was on wheels in less than 100 years after he was born. And how could anyone have imagined that Thomas Edison's inventions would be worth billions of dollars to mankind even before his 84 years on earth came to an end? Alexander Graham Bell died at 75, but not before he had launched the world into a new age of communications.

But mankind's greatest benefits have not come from inventors. Material conveniences offer no solutions to men's deepest problems. In some cases, they contribute to the complexity of the search for truth and peace.

If the Bible teaches anything, it teaches that those who have done the most for mankind have done it in the realm of the religious. And the quill has often been the sharpest instrument of their contribution. Take Moses for example. I doubt that all the pharaohs of Egypt combined made as great a contribution to the well-being of mankind as he. The strength of his character and the power of his pen have influenced millions of people for good and for God for 3,500 years.

Though no inventions are credited to Daniel, the power of his religious convictions influenced two world empires; and the inspiration of his quill continues to challenge millions of people 2,500 years after his death.

And how does one measure the 2,000-year influence for good and God of Paul's writings? We would not have had a Martin Luther without Paul. Nor would we have had the world's great Protestant nations without Luther.

Luther's "little tiff with the Pope" was far more than that. It was a conflict unto death in defense of the truth. Like Daniel, Luther was prepared to be thrown to the lions rather than deny the Word of God as he understood it. Thousands have followed in his footsteps.

Thank God for the quills of Moses, Paul, Luther, Knox, Calvin, and a hundred thousand others whose writings have strengthened the faith of believers and put the enemy to flight.

20
WHAT MORE?

WHAT IF . . .

"Somehow I expected Jesus to say more than, 'His sins are forgiven. Take him away!' "

There he was, flat on his back, and medical science had no answer for his physical need. You could not help being stirred by his pathetic condition. At least his four neighbors could not. So, they did something about it. They carried him to the Healer. They were sure that if their sick friend could only be made to walk and work, his problems would be solved.

Apparently the palsied man's four friends, along

with others who witnessed this event, had forgotten that the vast majority of the world's population is made up of people who walk and work, and yet have deep inner needs for which good health has no answer. They were surprised, therefore, to have Jesus give attention to the man's sin problem before responding to his health problem.

At any rate, Jesus did not argue about the pros and cons of the social gospel. He immediately put His finger on the man's deepest need. With a six-word thrust, He healed him of sin's malignancy—"Son, thy sins be forgiven thee" (Mark 2:5).

It is not incidental that in introducing Jesus to the world the angel said, "Thou shalt call His name *Jesus*, for He shall save His people from their sins" (Matt. 1:21). He did not say anything about saving them from their health problems.

John the Baptist said, "Behold the Lamb of God, which taketh away the sin of the world" (John 1:29). He did not say anything about taking away the world's poverty.

Jesus described the purpose of His coming in these words, "For the Son of man is come to seek and to save that which was lost" (Luke 19:10). He did not say He had come to educate the illiterate.

It is not that Christ or true believers in Him are indifferent to man's physical, material, and academic needs. He repeatedly demonstrated His concern for those aspects of man's welfare, and so has the Church. Rescue missions, orphanages, hospitals, and educational facilities around the world prove this. It is simply that the Saviour put first things first, and He has commanded His Church to do the same.

All of the world's social, academic, and economic needs are symptoms of the real problem—sin.

"Thy sins be forgiven thee" is the true Gospel. It is the only Good News for both time and eternity.

All of man's health, education, and welfare falls short of his ultimate need. Until his sin is forgiven and his heart changed, he cannot possibly use the academic, material, and social benefits that are his for the glory of God. As long as greed, lust, hate, envy, and a thousand and one other demons plague his heart, he cannot be really happy.

with others who witnessed this event, had forgotten that the vast majority of the world's population is made up of people who walk and work, and yet have deep inner needs for which good health has no answer. They were surprised, therefore, to have Jesus give attention to the man's sin problem before responding to his health problem.

At any rate, Jesus did not argue about the pros and cons of the social gospel. He immediately put His finger on the man's deepest need. With a six-word thrust, He healed him of sin's malignancy—"Son, thy sins be forgiven thee" (Mark 2:5).

It is not incidental that in introducing Jesus to the world the angel said, "Thou shalt call His name *Jesus*, for He shall save His people from their sins" (Matt. 1:21). He did not say anything about saving them from their health problems.

John the Baptist said, "Behold the Lamb of God, which taketh away the sin of the world" (John 1:29). He did not say anything about taking away the world's poverty.

Jesus described the purpose of His coming in these words, "For the Son of man is come to seek and to save that which was lost" (Luke 19:10). He did not say He had come to educate the illiterate.

It is not that Christ or true believers in Him are indifferent to man's physical, material, and academic needs. He repeatedly demonstrated His concern for those aspects of man's welfare, and so has the Church. Rescue missions, orphanages, hospitals, and educational facilities around the world prove this. It is simply that the Saviour put first things first, and He has commanded His Church to do the same.

All of the world's social, academic, and economic needs are symptoms of the real problem—sin.

"Thy sins be forgiven thee" is the true Gospel. It is the only Good News for both time and eternity.

All of man's health, education, and welfare falls short of his ultimate need. Until his sin is forgiven and his heart changed, he cannot possibly use the academic, material, and social benefits that are his for the glory of God. As long as greed, lust, hate, envy, and a thousand and one other demons plague his heart, he cannot be really happy.

21
OUT OF WINE?

WHAT IF . . .

"If I have to invite that itinerant Preacher and all His fishermen friends to my wedding, I'll be the laughingstock of Cana!"

Though Miriam's handwritten wedding invitations were short, her list of guests was long. It even included the young Carpenter from Nazareth, His mother, and a number of His followers.

Typical of Eastern weddings, the ceremony was both festive and long. And before Miriam and Amos were pronounced man and wife, an embarrassing shadow fell over the whole affair. That which contributed toward and symbolized the joy of the event (wine) was depleted. The caterer's frantic efforts to remedy the situation were of no avail. Cana's few small wine shops had been drained dry.

Neither Miriam, nor the mother of the Carpenter, nor any of the wedding guests could have guessed that such a situation would arise to mar an otherwise delightful event. Jesus alone had foreseen it. His acceptance of the invitation was doubtless based in part on that knowledge. He was always seeking to lift people out of problems for which they had no answer. In doing so, He demonstrated God's love for people.

I am glad Miriam and Amos invited the Carpenter to their wedding. He belongs at the wedding and in the home of every believer. And He has a way of making things right when He is there.

But I am concerned about how much we would have missed if Miriam and Amos (or whatever their names might have been) had not invited Jesus to their wedding. Not the least of our losses would have been Mary's statement to the servants, *"Whatsoever He saith unto you, do it"* (John 2:5). That so-packed-with-meaning command became the catalyst for the miracle in Cana's most memorable wedding. But that is not all. It has been the key to unnumbered miracles since. Obedience to that command has changed multitudes of problems to privileges in the lives of myriads of believers.

And what a message those six easily understood words have today for any believer, for any wedding, any home, any church, any business. Water has a way of changing to wine when we do what God tells us. Crooked ways seem to straighten out, and rough paths have a way of becoming smooth when we obey Him.

The open sesame to blessing is obedience. Whether we are to fill vessels with water, wash in the Pool of Siloam, lay aside our fishing nets, preach the Gospel to the farthest reaches of the earth, or to lose our life for His sake, there is no substitute for obedience. We either obey and rejoice in the consequences or disobey and run out of wine.

22
A RADICAL BOOK?

WHAT IF . . .

"Radical!"

In this fast-changing world of ours, the life expectancy of most books is less than six months. Even government restrictions that have been carefully thought out have ways of becoming obsolete very quickly.

Some of the regulations governing the operation of aircraft in the 1920s sound a little stupid today:

1. Don't take the machine into the air unless you are satisfied it will fly.

2. Pilots should carry hankies in a handy position to wipe off goggles.

3. In case the engine fails on take-off, land straight ahead regardless of obstacles.

4. If you see another machine near you, get out of its way.

5. Do not trust altitude instruments.

Sounds way out, doesn't it? There is something about our sophisticated, 700-miles-an-hour planes of today that makes it all look irrelevant.

Though the newest books of the Bible were written more than 1,800 years ago, they seem to have a way of saying something to the man or woman who studies them today. How is one to account for the fact that the message of the Bible is so pertinent and applicable?

One answer is that the character of God does not change. His character consists of absolutes: absolute holiness, absolute righteousness, absolute faithfulness, absolute love, etc. The principles spelled out in the Bible are a reflection of those absolutes. That is why the Ten Commandments, written 3,500 years ago, and the Sermon on the Mount, preached almost 2,000 years ago, are so meaningful today. Some things are never right to do in any generation in any country. Other things are never right to leave undone. The Ten Commandments, like the invariable speed of light, are never apt to become outmoded.

Another reason God's Word is pertinent today is that the nature of man does not change. Customs and cultures vary; communication and education may improve or fail; economic conditions fluctuate; but the moral nature of man remains the same. Lying, stealing, hating, envying, and killing are not inventions of the 20th century. No generation has ever been without them.

The Bible more than any other book has a way of uncovering the character of both God and man. In it the sharp contrast between the two comes into instant focus, and man's greatest need lies naked and exposed before his eyes. Then the Bible has a way of putting it all together. In the Bible man's need is revealed as God's opportunity, and the love of God in Christ solves the problem. A deep and radical change takes place, and other books become comparatively irrelevant to the true believer.

23
HOW TO BE WISER THAN YOUR TEACHERS

WHAT IF . . .

"Solomon, you're not listening!"

You do not have to be Solomon to be wiser than your teachers. You may never be more knowledgeable than some of your professors, but you can be wiser. Cramming your 12 billion brain cells with information is vastly different from having the ability to make right choices. And *there* is the rub. Life is a daily stream of choices, and the wise man is he who makes the right ones.

The psalmist tells us that true wisdom springs from the soil of a right attitude toward God. Or, in his words, "The fear of the Lord is the beginning of wisdom" (Ps. 111:10). All the information on earth apart from reverence for Almighty God falls short of wisdom. And when one contemplates the fact that God alone is omniscient, it makes sense to believe that a right relationship with Him is the alpha of wisdom.

The psalmist said that because he loved the law of God and meditated on it day and night, it made him wiser than his enemies and gave him more understanding than his teachers (Ps. 119:97-99). And who was there in David's day whose wisdom could put a lie to his testimony? Have the lives or writings of any who lived 3,000 years ago been more meaningful than those of the psalmist?

From whence did Solomon get a wisdom that exceeded that of all the kings of the earth? The answer goes back to a little dialogue between God and the king.

God: "Now that you are king of Israel, what would you like to have Me give you?"

Solomon: "Give therefore Thy servant an understanding heart to judge Thy people, that I may discern between good and bad."

God: "Behold, I have done according to thy words. Lo, I have given thee a wise and an understanding heart, so that there was none like thee before thee, neither after thee shall any arise like unto thee" (1 Kings 3).

From that day to this, Solomon's wisdom has been

proverbial, and his proverbs have been a source of wisdom in many countries and languages. Then One greater than Solomon came along who was the very wisdom and righteousness of God. Wise men sought Him at the time of His birth, and wise men have been both seeking and following Him ever since.

The teachings of the philosophers are pallid and insipid when compared to Christ's Sermon on the Mount or His supreme statement of all that is important in life, "Thou shalt love the Lord thy God with all thy heart, and with all thy soul, and with all thy strength, and with all thy mind; and thy neighbor as thyself" (Luke 10:27).

It is little wonder that the Holy Spirit used Paul's quill to write, "For the wisdom of this world is foolishness with God" (1 Cor. 3:19). Happy, therefore, is the man who seeks first the kingdom of God and His righteousness, for he will be wiser than his teachers.

24
WHAT'S IN YOUR SOUL-WINNER'S KIT?

WHAT IF . . .

"I see you've been discussing theology in the barber shop again!"

"It's not so much what you say,
As the manner in which you say it.
It's not so much the language you use,

as the tone in which you convey it."

It is alarmingly possible to win an argument and lose a soul. Apparently one's academic *aptitude* in presenting Gospel truths in logical sequence is somewhat less important than one's *attitude* of love toward the person to whom the truth is presented.

It is not surprising that our best lessons on witnessing come from the life of our Lord. To sit with Him as He talks with Nicodemus is to learn how to communicate to the deeply religious. Read Christ's straightforward yet gentle words as He speaks to the highly trained mind and heart of this honest doubter (see John 3:1-21).

To walk with Jesus to Jacob's well in Sychar and to listen to His patient conversation with the troubled Samaritan woman is to witness the kind of compassion that wins burdened people to the love of God (see John 4).

Watch Jesus as He sends the blind man to the Pool of Siloam to wash. Listen to the man, now seeing, as he argues with the Pharisees concerning how his healing came about. Then watch again as the Lord seeks him out and asks, "Do you believe on the Son of God?" When the unnamed recipient of sight asks who the Son of God is that he might believe, Jesus replies, "You have seen Him, and it is He who is speaking with you."

"Lord, I believe," is the quick and happy response (see John 9:35-38).

Perhaps a return trip to Jericho's tree-lined main street will also help us. There Jesus is stopping to speak to a man up a tree. "Come on down, Zaccheus. I want to have lunch with you," He says. And whatever else this master soul-winner said to the despised tax collector was wonderfully effective. Zaccheus becomes a new man, and all of that without debate or argument (see Luke 19:1-10).

There is, of course, a difference between being meek in one's witness and being weak. The early believers prayed for courage as they witnessed despite persecution and imprisonment. Paul faced opposition more than once while proclaiming the Gospel. At Athens he was verbally attacked by the Stoic and Epicurean philosophers, who called him a babbler and mocked at his faith in the resurrection of Christ. But through it all, Paul maintained his spiritual equilibrium, and as a result "certain men clave unto him and believed" (Acts 17:34).

James tells us that true wisdom is "first pure, then peaceable, gentle, and easy to be entreated, full of mercy and good fruits, without partiality, and without hypocrisy" (James 3:17). Doubtless this is the kind of wisdom we need in sharing the love of God with others. A pure motive, a heart full of peace, a gentle manner, a listening ear, a compassionate spirit, and a good life are about the best tools a man can carry in his soul-winning kit.

25
LISTEN, STONEHEAD!

WHAT IF . . .

"I said, 'We forgive you!'"

An American corporal in World War I single-handedly killed 20 Germans and forced 132 others to surrender. Though he received the Congressional Medal of Honor for his deed, he can probably not be named by one American in a million today.

Three thousand years ago a Jewish teen-ager killed a Philistine soldier, and millions of people around the world can repeat the important aspects of that famous victory.

So, why should a story out of antiquity be better known than a contemporary one? Certainly the American soldier's exploit was no less dramatic than David's, and there is no lack of access to World War I history.

Interesting, isn't it, that no duel in all history has captured the imagination of so many people for so many centuries in so many languages as the one fought between David and Goliath. Artists have pictured it, preachers have expounded it, and authors have written about it. Mothers have read it to their children, young people have been inspired by it, and scoffers have mocked it.

Far beyond all that, it has brought spiritual help to thousands. Honest obedience to its message has changed empty profession to happy possession and frustration to fruitfulness in many lives.

I am glad David did not compromise with the enemy. In fact, compromise is a form of surrender, and David could not reconcile giving one foot of territory to an enemy who insisted on defying and blaspheming God. Thanks, David.

Here are a few lessons we can learn from the lad who did the unpretentious thing of picking up five smooth stones:

1. His conflict came in the line of duty. He was not looking for a fight; but when it showed up, he was ready for it.

2. He had won lesser victories, and each victory gave him more faith for the next battle.

3. He used a weapon of proven value. David wisely rejected the king's armor and sword in favor of his trusted sling. Victory cannot be borrowed. It comes only to those who are disciplined in the use of the weapons God has entrusted to them.

4. The bright light of David's faith in God must

have blinded Goliath. It does something good to me just to let his words, "This day will the Lord deliver thee into mine hand," reverberate in my heart (see 1 Sam. 17:46).

5. Behind David's great exploit was an overriding determination that the God of Israel's armies should be glorified. And I suppose one cannot have a higher motive for any kind of victory than the glorification of God.

Let's get on with it.

26
HOW TO KILL A MISSIONARY

WHAT IF . . .

"Paul, we're delighted you could come to Corinth! If we hurry we'll be just in time for you to teach the Men's Bible Class. We have you scheduled for our youth rally this afternoon and for a question-and-answer period at the family-night supper to night. And, of course, the Women's Missionary Union will want to see your pictures."

Whatever you do, do not allow a missionary on furlough to become lazy. Keep him busy. That is the way he likes it. The 52 Sundays of his furlough year give you unprecedented opportunities to put him to work.

If at all possible, start him out with the 7 A.M. deacons' and elders' prayer meeting. If you do not already have one, then initiate it on the Sunday he arrives. It will let him know how prayerful the church is.

Make sure your missionary is given 10 minutes to speak in each of the four departments of the Sunday school. Then during the opening portion of the morning church service, you can have him speak at primary and junior churches. His speaking time in the adult service should be limited to three minutes. He is probably not a very good speaker.

After the noon meal (and make it good as he will not get anything else to eat for a couple of hours), ply him with questions. He just loves to tell you all about what the natives wear in his adopted country. You should also invite him to speak at the 3:30 P.M. meeting in the retirement home.

You will, of course, have lined him up to speak to the high school kids at 6:30 P.M. Give him seven minutes to show his slides in the evening service. Then round out his day by having him rap with the college young people from 9-11 P.M. He will never forget all you have done to keep him busy during the day.

Incidentally, do not tell him what his assignments are until five minutes before he is to speak. This injects a surprise element into his ministry. And when it comes to offerings, forget it. He is learning to live by faith anyway.

Of course, you cannot kill a missionary just by keeping him busy on Sundays, If he is going to be in your area for a few weeks, do your best to line him up with home Bible study classes, women's missionary circles, social study classes in the local grade schools, hospital visitation, and men's noonday luncheons.

You may find some of the best open doors for your furloughed missionary in distant towns. However, in deference to his health, you ought not to arrange meetings that are more than 800 miles apart. Fifteen hours of driving can become tiresome.

Make sure that your missionary's last week in America before returning to his field of service is well filled with social events. Do not let him leave with any feeling that he is being neglected by his church friends. Then, too, parties and dinners have a way of helping him forget all the last minute packing he should be doing.

By the way, if you do not hear from him for three months after he gets back on the field, maybe he is recuperating.

27
PRAYERS MINUS PIETY EQUALS NOTHING

WHAT IF . . .

"Boy, can she recite the Bible!"

Morals and modesty are as much a part of the Christian message as rituals and readings. But how easily we divorce them. Lung-destroying nicotine, liver-destroying alcohol, and lust-enticing fashions are much at home in many church circles. Sexual permissiveness, marital unfaithfulness, unclean verbal expletives, and business dishonesty all sit in padded church pews and rub shoulders with hymn-singing, Bible-reading, knee-bending people.

When was the last time you saw the pulpit of your church stand on its tiptoes and speak out against behavior patterns that are contrary to the plain teaching of the Bible? There are young people in our churches today who have never been exposed to the biblical standards of morality. They have watched a sex-crazed world cut the dress patterns into which Christian women have fitted all too comfortably. They have seen the miniskirt raise the rape ratio and wondered why the church has been so silent.

Of course, negative preaching for the sake of negative preaching is obviously negative. But a return to the "thou shalt not" teaching of God's Word is much needed. We need to restore the power of negative thinking.

All that is in the world, says the Bible, is the lust of the flesh, the lust of the eye, and the pride of life. It is little wonder that in such an atmosphere the Word of God gives much space and time to setting standards of speech, morals, modesty, honesty, and general behavior patterns. Strong teaching against all forms of sin and iniquity fills its pages. Furthermore, it clearly outlines the path of victory over every pitfall.

The quoting of Scripture verses and the singing of Gospel songs are hollow exercises when not backed by holiness. That worship of God that is not accompanied by a walk of godliness is hypocrisy. Religious convictions without holiness of character are vain.

When Jesus said, "Blessed are the pure in heart, for they shall see God," He put His finger on a captivating paradox. Without the "washing of the water of God's Word" the heart cannot be kept clean. On the other hand, man cannot see God in the Bible or anywhere else if his heart is filled with unclean desires or imaginations.

28

DO YOU KNOW THE AUTHOR'S NAME?

WHAT IF . . .

"Let's see . . . 'Bible,' 'Bible' . . . Do you know the author's name?"

"Billy, do you know the names of the first twins mentioned in the Bible?"

"Yes, Teacher. They were First and Second Samuel."

That bit of biblical illiteracy is really not funny in that it probably comes close to characterizing the ignorance of much of the world's population concerning the world's most widely sold book. In contrast, there is a homey bit of poetry that says,

"I entered the world's great library doors:
I crossed their acres of polished floors;
I searched and searched their stacks and nooks,
But I settled at last on the Book of books."

Apparently many others have felt just that way. Patrick Henry said, "This is a book worth all other books that were ever printed."

Robert E. Lee said, "The Bible is a book in comparison with which all other books are of minor importance."

Abraham Lincoln called it "the best gift God has given to man."

King David said, "The law of the Lord is perfect, converting the soul; the testimony of the Lord is sure, making wise the simple. The statutes of the Lord are right, rejoicing the heart; the commandment of the Lord is pure, enlightening the eyes. The fear of the Lord is clean, enduring forever; the judgments of the Lord are true and righteous altogether. More to be desired are they than gold, yea, than much fine gold; sweeter also than honey and the honeycomb. Moreover by them is thy servant warned; in keeping of them there is great reward" (Ps. 19:7-11).

Paul encouraged Timothy to forever remember that from childhood he had known the holy Scriptures which were able to make him wise unto salvation and to fully equip him for every good work.

An unknown author has written the following:

"The Bible contains the mind of God, the state of man, the way of salvation, the doom of sinners, and the happiness of believers. It has light to direct you, food to support you, and comfort to cheer you.

"It is the traveler's map, pilgrim's staff, pilot's compass, soldier's sword, and Christian's charter. It is a mine of wealth, paradise of glory, and river of pleasure.

"Its doctrines are holy, precepts binding, histories true, and decisions immutable. Christ is its grand subject, our good its design, and the glory of God its end.

"Read it to be wise, believe it to be safe, and practice it to be holy. It should fill the memory, rule the heart, and guide the feet.

"It is given you in life, will be opened at the judgment, and remembered forever. It involves the highest responsibility, will reward the greatest labor, and will condemn all who trifle with its so sacred contents."

John tells us the Bible was written "that ye might believe that Jesus is the Christ, the Son of God; and that believing ye might have life through His name" (John 20:31).

What a Book! What an Author!

29
A REAL EXPERIENCE

WHAT IF . . .

"We like to think of it as entering into what makes possible human existence with such momentum of delight and valuing that we are awakened and enabled to take part in world forming from the inside."

My name is Joel, son of Meshach, and I have just had the greatest religious experience of my life. I have been worshiping the golden calf. Believe me, I have never before felt such a spirit of unity among God's people. We have been singing together, dancing, feasting, praying, and playing. I guess you would call it an experience in *togetherness*.

One of the reasons this experience has meant so much to my wife and me is because we put a lot in it. She and hundreds of other wives gave their jewelry in order that we might have the calf to worship. I killed my best bull to offer as a sacrifice and to provide food for our love feast. I have learned the excitement of giving.

Of course, we do not really pray to the golden calf. We pray to the spirit of service it represents. After all, we could not have gotten this far in our wilderness journey without a lot of faithful oxen to serve us. We know the unseen God has given oxen to us, and this is our way of expressing our thanks. The whole spiritual experience was tremendous, and I intend to keep on enjoying it.

Moses and his crowd argue that what we are doing is contrary to the Word of God. He seems to think we are twisting the Word by our experience. He is almost rabid on the idea that we should evaluate our experience in the light of God's Word. But how do you argue with success? Look at the number of people who are enjoying this great religious exercise with my wife and me.

We look upon ourselves as religious existentialists, and I am sure we have what people really want. They do not want a set of principles. They want live, warm religious experience; and in our group, they are getting it. Of course, an experience without guidelines might lead every man to do what is right in his own eyes, and that could be confusing and divisive. It might even lead to the forming of various sects and denominations. But this will not happen in our group.

You can evaluate your spiritual experience by the truth, if you want to. In doing so, you will bypass a lot of exciting situations. As for me and

29
A REAL EXPERIENCE

WHAT IF . . .

"We like to think of it as entering into what makes possible human existence with such momentum of delight and valuing that we are awakened and enabled to take part in world forming from the inside."

My name is Joel, son of Meshach, and I have just had the greatest religious experience of my life. I have been worshiping the golden calf. Believe me, I have never before felt such a spirit of unity among God's people. We have been singing together, dancing, feasting, praying, and playing. I guess you would call it an experience in *togetherness*.

One of the reasons this experience has meant so much to my wife and me is because we put a lot in it. She and hundreds of other wives gave their jewelry in order that we might have the calf to worship. I killed my best bull to offer as a sacrifice and to provide food for our love feast. I have learned the excitement of giving.

Of course, we do not really pray to the golden calf. We pray to the spirit of service it represents. After all, we could not have gotten this far in our wilderness journey without a lot of faithful oxen to serve us. We know the unseen God has given oxen to us, and this is our way of expressing our thanks. The whole spiritual experience was tremendous, and I intend to keep on enjoying it.

Moses and his crowd argue that what we are doing is contrary to the Word of God. He seems to think we are twisting the Word by our experience. He is almost rabid on the idea that we should evaluate our experience in the light of God's Word. But how do you argue with success? Look at the number of people who are enjoying this great religious exercise with my wife and me.

We look upon ourselves as religious existentialists, and I am sure we have what people really want. They do not want a set of principles. They want live, warm religious experience; and in our group, they are getting it. Of course, an experience without guidelines might lead every man to do what is right in his own eyes, and that could be confusing and divisive. It might even lead to the forming of various sects and denominations. But this will not happen in our group.

You can evaluate your spiritual experience by the truth, if you want to. In doing so, you will bypass a lot of exciting situations. As for me and my house, we are a bit more pragmatic. Our faith is in an experience we can feel. Or should I say, a bull we can touch.

30

THE GREAT COMMISSION OR THE GREAT CONFUSION?

WHAT IF . . .

"Go ye into all the world and exegete a faithful theology of mobility, independence, and creativity on which to predicate action (program-mission) that is receivable as good news by those living the contemporary urban life-style."

There He sat, surrounded by 11 incredulous men munching on broiled fish. The miracle of His resurrection was slowly breaking through into their minds. "And now," He said, "I want you to start here in Jerusalem, and then move on into other areas and nations, preaching the Gospel to everyone."

"Peter, Thomas, and the rest of you—you understand what repentance and remission of sins means, don't you? Repentance includes being sorry for and turning from your sin. You have experienced that. Remittance means payment, and you understand that I have paid the price for man's sins. Forgiveness is his for the asking. This is the Good News I want you to proclaim. Do you get the picture?"

Silence you could hear filled the room. Then a bit hesitantly John spoke, "But, Master, don't man's deepest needs lie in the field of the psychological? If we can get his thought patterns concerning himself and his fellowman straightened out, won't that do the job?"

"I don't agree with John for one moment," responded Peter. "Man's basic problems are found in the realm of the physical. Give him plenty of bread and butter and he will love God and others, too. Money solves a lot of problems, you know."

James was finding it difficult to keep still. "Gentlemen," he said, "you know as well as I that our people are more concerned about political issues than anything else. If we can be used of God to get this nation from under the Roman heel, we will accomplish the greatest thing on earth. I'm sure there are other subjugated people who feel the same way about the injustices they are suffering. It is law and order this old world needs."

"Friends, you are to be My witnesses. Your message is the story of My compassion for lost men," said Jesus. "My crucifixion and resurrection are the center and circumference of your proclamation to the world. I have come to seek and save the lost. I am the Lamb of God who takes away the sin of the world. There is no other name given under heaven through which men can be saved. I am the Truth of God, the Way of God, and the Life of God. You are My ambassadors."

Tears surfaced in John's eyes as he said, "Forgive us, Lord. God forbid that we should ever be satisfied to preach anything other than the truth of Your love for men. As for me and my house, we will never allow any philosophy or ism to obliterate the glory of Your supreme sacrifice and the wonder of Your resurrection."

Is that how it really happened? I don't know. But I do know what message the Twelve took out to a lost world. And I know it worked miracles of transformation.